Its All About THE DOUGH

A MODEL FOR THE FELLOWSHIP AMONG WOMEN

Amy Kemp

WESTBOW
PRESS®
A DIVISION OF THOMAS NELSON
& ZONDERVAN

Scripture taken from the Holy Bible, NEW INTERNATIONAL VERSION®.
Copyright © 1973, 1978, 1984 by Biblica, Inc. All rights reserved worldwide.
Used by permission. NEW INTERNATIONAL VERSION® and NIV® are
registered trademarks of Biblica, Inc. Use of either trademark for the offering
of goods or services requires the prior written consent of Biblica US, Inc.

All Scripture quotations in this publications are from The Message.
Copyright © by Eugene H. Peterson 1993, 1994, 1995, 1996, 2000,
2001, 2002. Used by permission of NavPress Publishing Group.

Scripture taken from the Contemporary English Version © 1991,
1992, 1995 by American Bible Society, Used by Permission.

WestBow Press books may be ordered through booksellers or by contacting:

WestBow Press
A Division of Thomas Nelson & Zondervan
1663 Liberty Drive
Bloomington, IN 47403
www.westbowpress.com
1 (866) 928-1240

Because of the dynamic nature of the Internet, any web addresses or links contained in
this book may have changed since publication and may no longer be valid. The views
expressed in this work are solely those of the author and do not necessarily reflect the
views of the publisher, and the publisher hereby disclaims any responsibility for them.

Any people depicted in stock imagery provided by Thinkstock are models,
and such images are being used for illustrative purposes only.
Certain stock imagery © Thinkstock.

ISBN: 978-1-5127-1728-0 (sc)
ISBN: 978-1-5127-1729-7 (e)

Library of Congress Control Number: 2015917377

Print information available on the last page.

WestBow Press rev. date: 10/23/2015

CONTENTS

INTRODUCTION

I remember sitting at The Cheesecake Factory in St. Louis with my daughter on a short trip one summer to visit a couple of colleges. We mixed that primary task with a little bonding time in the shopping mall. Famished from a day of fast-paced, store-to-store, dedicated shopping, the decor of the restaurant and its delectable name, The *Cheesecake* Factory, drew us in under its mystic spell. Although we were starving, we knew that a visit to *this* place wouldn't be a visit at all if we didn't save room for dessert. After clearing our half-eaten pizza and sandwich from the marble table top, our waitress presented us with a separate and distinctly calorie-careless dessert menu. Our eyes took in all of the options, our smiles widened, and our anticipation grew. Now these were *decadent* desserts! Despite our top-notch meals, we waited with anticipation for the final course—the one that would surely make us miserable as we wallowed in self-indulgence. Even in that moment, I thought, "Lord, wouldn't Your word about women and friendships be better likened to something like this *instead* of a simple chocolate chip cookie?" These desserts are served on fine China and deserve their very own menus. But, stronger and stronger grew a still, small voice convincing me to share *these words* in just *this way*. It had to be a chocolate chip cookie, plain and simple.

I've come to more fully appreciate the simplicity of the chocolate chip cookie. There are nine ingredients to this recipe—only nine! Try to make a red-wine velvet cake or tiramisu with just nine ingredients. I thought over each ingredient and how they come together. I considered the final product and how too much of one ingredient or too little of another can drastically affect the outcome—the taste, the texture, and appearance. Much can be learned from this nine-ingredient wonder. And, as women, I think that God offers this analogy because we need it in spoonfuls, just as cookies are dropped onto a lightly greased cookie sheet before entering the oven. We need understanding in sweet, consumable nuggets, not in mountains of richness and overindulgence. This friendship lesson should be uncomplicated and straightforward, a single bite at a time.

Each chapter of this book explores one ingredient in the simplest of chocolate chip cookie recipes. Eggs, baking soda, sugars, vanilla: each has a particular role to play. Maybe this life recipe analogy will be integral in helping us to pare down and strip away. As women, we may need to move forward with less and not more. Maybe what will be revealed is a mixture of sweetness, saltiness, and bitterness that leaves happiness, satisfaction, and contentment. Maybe what results is a recognition that we are surrounded with women who display the very characteristics that combine for enjoyment, refreshment, and cohesiveness—a near perfect recipe. But, these chapters might also be conviction that our recipes are incomplete. Are we missing crucial ingredients? Is our circle of influence like this simple dessert option? I hope so. Let's tie up our aprons, move to the pantry, and look at all of the ingredients necessary for this fabulous life recipe.

CHAPTER 1

Flour

As a child, I often watched *Little House on the Prairie*. Worlds away from the plethora of channels available to us from modern-day entertainment options (*Direct TV, Dish,* Netflix, or even cable), I knew my limitations. My home was equipped with a very old-fashioned, rusty, and mostly useless television antenna. It took less than 15 seconds to flip through the channels to determine what the TV had to offer once I'd thrown my backpack to the floor, grabbed a snack, and watched the school bus head down the dusty, country road to deliver the next students safely home. I'd pause every day on *Little House on the Prairie.* Through the "snowy" television screen (given the poor reception we had), I could see the Ingalls girls running down the grassy hillside as the musical interlude played in the background. Many a young girl in my generation likened herself to Laura Ingalls Wilder; I was no different. I was a tomboy, not afraid of hard work, and perhaps a bit too mischievous at times. I respected my parents, had high ambitions, and spent plenty of time outdoors. Although I didn't call my folks "ma" and "pa," there was much about Laura's on-screen life that seemed similar to mine. In my childhood, in the 1970s, I became Laura Ingalls Wilder in my living room after school each day.

In the long-running series, Nellie Olsen was Laura's nemesis in many ways. In Laura's eyes, Nellie was rich, excessively rich. Nellie's family owned and operated the mercantile. Laura, the poor country girl, could only afford the smallest, most insignificant of items in the Olsen Mercantile. She would save and save, just for a piece of hard candy from the candy jar. She, no doubt, learned frugality from her ma (Carolyn) and her pa (Charles). She watched their trips to the mercantile and learned from their experiences with the Olsen family. Ma and Pa might come with several dozen eggs to trade for other merchandise, and they always endured the scowl of Mrs. Olsen, Nellie's up-tight mother, who thought that her clientele ought to be of higher class than the Ingalls family.

I mention these characters and the setting of *Little House on the Prairie* because, as a child, the idea of a town mercantile fascinated me. Perhaps it was the precursor to our modern-day Wal-Mart and one-stop shopping. Although it was perhaps the only store in town, there were few conveniences to Olsen's Mercantile. Doing any sort of "trading" (eggs for flour, for example, as would have been done by Carolyn Ingalls), required that you hitch up the team and the buckboard so that you could haul home your purchased items. And forget about convenience items. Today, we've become spoiled by tidy portions marketed just perfectly for our needs. Want just a small drink? Sure, pick up an 8-oz soda can. Feeling a bit thirstier? Try the liter size. Having company? Why not pick up a 24-pack of your favorite. We get things just the way that we like them. But, this was not true in the days of Laura Ingalls. Quantities of flour hauled home from the mercantile were packaged in large, durable bags, perhaps weighing over 100 lbs when filled to the brim. Why so much? Laura Ingalls would tell you it was because Ma made everything with that flour: pie crusts, pancakes, noodles, biscuits, cookies, bread. Flour was a necessary staple and a practicality for pioneer living.

If our lives are vessels for combining the ingredients of a chocolate chip cookie, then let me suggest that plain-old, utilitarian flour is a must-have. Take a look at any chocolate chip cookie recipe; the ingredient called for in the highest quantity is flour. The concept is simple: no flour, no cookies. How many ladies have looked through a recipe book at this concoction or that mixture, poking around at what they might or might not be able to fix from the items in their pantry only to be disappointed that the dust left at the bottom of an empty flour canister isn't enough to bake up any treat whatsoever? You just <u>have to have</u> flour. In fact, in the Midwest, most women would claim that their pantries are incomplete without this one commodity from the mercantile. Flour is utilitarian; it's *functional*. And functional is synonymous with practical, purposeful, and sensible. It is the base ingredient for countless goodies we enjoy eating, not just cookies. We need flour.

Similarly, life is incomplete without surface-level, practical, and purposeful friends; we'll call them the flour in our lives. If flour in a cookie provides bulk; surface-level friends, acquaintances, and neighbors in our lives provide depth. They make life substantive. When taking inventory of our friendships, we should find many of these floury individuals. Their roles in our lives are practical. These ladies share carpool responsibilities to get our kids to and from school each day. They sit beside us at church on Sundays. They attend our aerobics class or show up at story hour at the library at just the same time we're dropping our kids off at the front door. We know them, perhaps in a superficial way. We make small talk with them. We share in commonalities. And, ladies, we need a lot of them.

Don't be lead astray at this point, pondering, "Wait. I can't maintain hundreds of friendships! Life is too busy, too complicated." That's right. Great value is found in simply maintaining healthy, surface relationships. As women, too often we are caught up in believing that we need to deepen relationships and foster more intimate one-on-one interactions. Not so. Special friends are close sisters. Special friends share confidentialities and are warmly and affectionately connected to us. They are intimate comrades. But, in this life recipe, those special friends are not flour. They have a different role to play. Limiting such special, intimate friendships is healthy, in fact. Use the example that

Jesus provided. He had three intimate companions. Peter, James, and John were his go-to guys. Much different are our floury, practical friends. Plainly, they don't require as much time and energy. Practical relationships require minimal maintenance. Don't spread yourself too thin. Recognize that "floury" friends are a solid foundation for you; they are essential.

I learned a poignant lesson about the essential nature of floury friends from a commencement speaker years ago. When my eldest daughter graduated from the eighth grade, one of the teachers in her school, a highly decorated instructor who had been recognized among other educators at The White House that spring, was the guest speaker. I remember her illustration during that ceremony.

The teacher talked about the transition from elementary school to high school. She held up a thick textbook. My guess was that this book was from her college days. The hard-bound volume could have easily served as a door stop and a simultaneous toe-breaker should you mis-step. It was clearly heavy. She challenged all of those watching and listening to guess at whether simple cardstock paper, when rolled into a cylinder and taped together, could withstand the extreme weight of that text; could the paper hold up the book? The eighth graders were specifically asked to respond. And, they responded negatively. It couldn't. No way. This wise educator then likened that heavy textbook to the upcoming high school experience upon which these students were about to embark. It would be a heavy one. There would be more homework, more extra-curricular activities, more peer choices, more adolescent trials, and more drama. One piece of plain cardstock (an individual student) rolled into a cylinder could not withstand that kind of environment. To illustrate, she set the book squarely on top of that cardstock and within an instant, the book came slamming onto the table, crushing the cardstock below. But, in her wisdom, this master educator went on to assure the students they weren't alone.

She cut a piece of the cardstock, rolled it into the size of a toilet paper tube, and said, "When times get tough, you'll have your good friends." She sat that cylinder on the table. She said, "You'll have your teachers," as she rolled a second cylinder from another half-sheet of cardstock, taped it together, and placed it on the table. She said, "You'll have your guidance counselor, your parents, and your church," and she placed three more smaller cylinders of rolled cardstock onto the table. And then, to prove her point well, she carefully and very gingerly laid that weighty book down on all of those cylinders simultaneously, and they stood tall. Point proven. Well done, Master Teacher.

Those eighth grade students walked away understanding that the road ahead wouldn't be easy, but they could share it with many and survive. We can learn from that same lesson. Life isn't easy. Without a wide array of friends to help bear the load, we might stumble and fall. We might even be crushed. However, the more we band with others, even in surface relationships, the more strength we have to endure daily life.

CHAPTER 2

Baking Soda

Colossians 2:9-10 (New International Version) says, "For in Christ, all the fullness of the Deity lives in bodily form, and in Christ, you have been brought to *fullness*." So, how full do you feel?

I love the holidays. Beginning with the first cool streak in September or October, every fiber in my being wants to run to my kitchen and bake, bake, bake. Crank up the oven, set the TV to a college football game so that I can hear the announcers call the play-by-play, and tie up my apron. Those are great days in the kitchen. As a young girl, I have fond memories of baking cookies with my grandmother in her kitchen. She loved warm cookies. She'd say if your tongue could stand the heat, they were best straight from the oven. She had such a tiny, tiny kitchen. Literally, you pulled the table out into the main floor from its tidy place in the corner of the room to eat your meal. Countertop space? Phhhft. Maybe a three-foot section, but that was cluttered with dingy green

Tupperware® canisters, a candy dish (mostly for my pappy, who loved chocolate), and the daily mail. Space didn't matter. We could make heaven-on-earth creations from that little culinary haven, regardless of the inconveniences. With a kitchen that small, it didn't take much for sweet aromas to inundate the whole place. There was no mistaking baking days; the sweet smells likely wafted out of the open kitchen windows, notifying neighbors of the fun going on inside. Maybe it is the thought of that tiny little kitchen, the aromatic environment, and the heat generated by the trusty gas stove that make me want to fatten up my own family with sweets each fall.

If that desire of mine only stopped when the snow fall started, though. When the weather turns even colder, my motherly provider persona kicks into overdrive. I dig out not only the pumpkin and apple recipes from fall, but the sugar cookie cookbook and the holiday meal guide. I plan out when I'll make what candy treat and for whom. I even plan weekday evenings when I can complete a half-batch of this or accomplish step one of that so that I can get all of it done while balancing a full-time job, school, and church activities. My husband calls me his saboteur. (I'm a little embarrassed to tell you that I originally thought that was a compliment. I wanted to believe that I was a good wife for piling on these goodies from October through December until I realized he had confounded me with his 50-cent vocabulary.) He struggles with overindulging, particularly sweets. Don't we all? And, here I was enabling him to eat his way into a sugar coma. I just want my family to feel satisfied and to enjoy warm food in a warm home, knowing they are warmly loved.

That's the kind of "fullness" I think of when I read the passage from Colossians. "You have been brought to fullness." Are we satisfied in Christ? Are we full? If our life's recipe is a little flat, then perhaps it is missing a distinctly "filling" ingredient: baking soda. If you're not a kitchen guru and baking's not your thing, then you might be thinking, "Isn't soda in a golden box with some strapping man's bicep on the logo?" Yep. It is. On the surface, it doesn't look a lot different than flour, but its effect on the recipe is unmistakable. It is a leavening agent, meaning it causes the dough to rise while in the oven. Without baking soda, cookies would be flat, thick-textured, and much less satisfying. Baking soda is the key to fullness in chocolate chip cookies.

Let me share a story about the friend who introduced me to this fullness concept. I came to know JudiJo when we served a church together for a season of our lives. At the time, our children were very close to the same age, and we shared many similarities. JudiJo's personality was bubbly. Very rarely was that woman seen without a smile on her face. Spend any time with her at all, and you'd learn quickly that she loved her boys (she had two), she loved her husband, and she loved to cook. Dedicated to the new church plant our families were serving, we bathed that new body of Christ in prayer continually. And, what prayer meeting is complete without a little refreshment—a container of cookies, chips and dip, maybe a sandwich or two? Sunday evening prayer groups and fellowship times might travel from home to home, but rest assured whatever JudiJo brought to the table was likely the first dish consumed at those meetings. She enjoyed "filling" people. Her joy bubbled over.

When I was a young girl there was a song that we'd sing in church camp about bubbling over. It was sung as a round. One group of children would repeat the mantra, "Bubblin' over. Bubblin' over. Bubblin' over." A second group would sing, "Jesus' love is bubblin' over. Jesus' love is bubblin' over." When you put it together, even with young, untrained voices, we sounded as though we were percolating in an old-fashioned coffee pot. Baking soda friends have so much of Christ's fullness in them that it bubbles over. They enjoy laughter and smiles, and they are quick to tell all those around them that the source of their joy is Jesus Christ.

My bubbly friend, JudiJo, lives miles away from me now. Her ministry with her husband has taken her to Tulsa, Oklahoma, far from my Illinois homestead, but I know she is the same JudiJo. She has a website from which I have cabbaged onto the absolute best turkey marinade for Thanksgiving Day among other recipes she has posted there. Yes, she's still filling people with her cooking skills, great recipes included. But, she is also still filling folks as a result of the fullness of Christ that bubbles over in her, too. I know this because though miles separate us, we are Facebook friends. Countless times, I have run across

JudiJo's posts in my news feed, and even without her image there, I think I could recognize her writing, and I know I could recognize what I've come to appreciate as her tagline. She'll post something about her sons, her husband, or God's provision and grace, and she'll conclude with one phrase that only a "baking soda" friend could use with such poignancy: "My heart is full." I know it is, JudiJo. I know it is.

Consider our lives as women and how we are mixed together with others around us. Who is bubbling over into us? Who is completing our recipe with the fullness of Christ in such a way that we are blessed because of it? Are we this ingredient in the life of another? Are we using opportunities to effervesce with joy and <u>fill</u> others' lives? We risk a very flat, thick existence without some baking soda. Don't miss it—either as a giver or a receiver.

CHAPTER 3

Salt

I was an English major in college. In fact, to make that fact even more ho-hum, I'll share the truth that I liked, maybe even loved, English grammar. Most folks shy far away from the oddities of English grammar. Whether it is a matter of too versus to or their, they're, and there, I know a host of friends who find out that I loved English grammar and immediately silence themselves for fear that they'll mis-step.

Perhaps one of the trickier word choices for me has always been affect versus effect. I have a grasp on the correct choice, but I have to run through the rules in my head before I put my pen to paper. Of one thing I'm sure, however: the next ingredient in the friendship recipe of women is effective! Salt. Just the tiniest dash changes flavor greatly.

I have a salt story or at least a salt memory. Growing up, most of my Sunday meals were big ones, and whether the main dish was fried pork chops, fried chicken, or fried steak (do you see a pattern here?), the accompanying dish was almost always mashed potatoes and gravy. Making milk gravy is a lost art. I'm convinced that fewer and fewer cooks today can assemble the right amount of drippings and flour to aid in the thickening before adding the main ingredient, milk. I still make it for my family once in a while, but the side dish was much more common in my childhood. Whether it was my mom or my grandmother, who was affectionately known as Mimmie in our home, one thing was certain, a good pan of gravy could only be produced with the right amount of salt. A salt shaker sat close to the burner on the stove top when the gravy-making exercise was in session. The pattern went like this: stir, stir, stir; turn over the back of the spoon; swipe your finger across the covered utensil, and taste. There would be a split-second pause for one's taste buds to catch up, but if the flavor wasn't just right, the salt shaker would soon be in action over the top of the boiling pan. I can almost see the steam, taste the goodness, and hear the rubbing of the spoon on the bottom of the skillet as I think back.

Then or now, no good country kitchen should be without salt, despite the health warnings that too much of it will result in high blood pressure. Salt has been an effective ingredient for centuries, and not just in tiny kitchens in the Midwest. Think back to those *Little House on the Prairie* days again. How was meat preserved? It was salted! Whether it was game that had been shot and killed on the prairie or a cow butchered for a large family to share, without refrigeration, the only way to preserve and make full use of the meat was to salt it.

Salt shows up in other ways as well. I am a runner. On a very hot summer day, even when I try to hydrate, I'll return home after a long run to see crystals on my shoulders and forehead...salt! My body has drawn out the moisture, and on the surface of my skin is the resulting salt. It is a sure sign of dehydration, not unlike dehydrated meat being preserved in days gone by.

Simply, salt is an ingredient that *effectively* makes all other ingredients come together. In the process of preservation, the salt draws all of the water out of the meat, making it dense. The practice actually makes the meat toxic to most bacteria! Imagine that: a matter so dense and so tightly bound that harm (in the form of bacteria) cannot come to it.

Now, the question in our relationships as ladies is: who is tightly bound to us?

When examining the women in our lives, we can generally identify the salty ones. They are the ladies that have the power to make other ingredients come together. These are your leader friends. These are the movers and the shakers (the salt shakers). These are the women who seem to always have the plan that will result in success. They are good leaders, too, not those who talk much and act little and not those who are disrespectful and judgmental on their way to the top. No, these are the ladies who are gifted by God Himself to tie friends around them tightly so that harm does not befall these women on their way to achieving a corporate goal.

Perhaps one of the greatest friendship examples in the scriptures is that of David and Jonathan. This unlikely twosome serves as an excellent model of bonded, impenetrable dedication to one another. From the Old Testament, we may remember that Jonathan was the son of King Saul, the same King Saul who pursued David with rage, vengeance, and the intent to kill. David hid from Saul time and time again, fleeing his wrath and fearing for his life. In I Samuel, Chapter 20, Jonathan and David are meeting in private. Jonathan, blind to his father's rage, wishes to bring comfort to David. Jonathan wants to believe that King Saul is not vile nor full of hatred as David believes. Jonathan's heart's desire and his deep friendship with David make him oblivious to the truth. Nonetheless, the two formulate a plan. It is the New Moon festival, and David's presence at the King's table will be requested. Jonathan, David's leader friend, will act as his salt. He will be present at the New Moon festival and if King Saul should ask as to the whereabouts of David, Jonathan will claim that David had asked permission to go to Bethlehem to celebrate with his brother. Saul's reaction to Jonathan's excuse will certainly reveal his true feelings.

So what happens? The Word says that Saul's "anger flared" (I Samuel 20:30, New International Version) to the point that King Saul hurls a spear at his own son, furious that Jonathan has sided with David and schemed to enable his escape. Later in the chapter Jonathan, again in secret, meets with David to share with him the truth that he now believes: King Saul does intend harm and will kill David if given the opportunity. David leaves the scene at the end of Chapter 20 and Jonathan goes back to town. End story. Just like that, the chapter concludes. There's no summary statement, no "happily ever after," and no resolution. That's hard to swallow when, as readers, we want this friendship to last indefinitely.

For me, the take-away from this account is that regardless of familial relationships, regardless of almost certain harm, and regardless of his own future, Jonathan remained bonded to David. He was devoted. He would stop at nothing, not even the wrath of his crazed father, to protect David. I've sometimes heard young people talk about their friendships, saying, "We're tight." They might even wrap their index finger and middle finger together to give a visual of what they mean with that phrase. When we look at this account of Jonathan and David, that word picture is very descriptive and spot-on: they were tight.

Again, what does salt do? It so <u>tightly</u> binds that it makes harmful substances incapable of preventing injury. This is what we've learned about its use in preservation. What had Jonathan done? He had unveiled the truth and had *protected his friend from harm.* His compassion for David was deep, his bond with David was strong, his commitment to his friend was impenetrable. Jonathan acted out every part of the plan to learn the truth (see all of I Samuel 20 for details), and he kept his commitment. The scripture says, "Then, they kissed each other and wept together" (I Samuel 20:41, New International Version). Ladies, if a woman doesn't have some salt in her life, she doesn't know commitment, or trust, or unity. These are things The Lord wants us to know and experience. Find salt. Be salt.

CHAPTER 4

Sugars

So integral to our friendship recipe is the sugary component that literally two different kinds need to be a part of the mix—white, granulated sugar and packed, brown sugar. There must be something important to learn about this sticky and highly craved ingredient.

Have you ever tried to eliminate sugar from a recipe? Maybe you just forgot it. It happens. It happened to my mom once. My daughter's absolute favorite pie is pumpkin. Knowing this, upon a visit to her "Nana's" house one fall day (the perfect climate for pumpkin), my mom (Nana) prepared in advance a creamy pumpkin pie to serve as a surprise. It was sure to be a delight to her granddaughter, Tess. I only wish that I had been a fly upon the wall to see it all unfold first-hand, but I can imagine. I can imagine my mom, with a smile upon her face, slicing a big portion of pie and placing it upon a small plate for Tess to enjoy. I can imagine her serving it graciously to this precious granddaughter, waiting for the smile to widen across her face as she enjoyed the richness of Nana's kitchen. I can imagine the anticipation my mom felt, knowing how satisfying it is to give from the heart a gift prepared by one's own hands. She had the assurance that THIS gift was just the right gift: a piece of sweet, creamy pumpkin goodness. These are the things that make the whole world better.

Then, I can imagine my daughter, Tess. This young one wouldn't dare criticize her nana, not for a thing. She could be served nearly anything at the hand of her nana and be thankful for the expression of love and generosity. Innocently, she sat and watched as the perfect-*looking* slice of heaven was lifted from the tin pie plate. Anticipation filled her mind as her stomach prepared for a treat that would surely satisfy. Nana's made her many treats before—Oreo dirt cake, Italian cream cake, fresh strawberries and ice cream—but, nothing is better to my Tess' tummy than the goodness of pumpkin pie. She awaits the first bite, eyes closed, palette prepared. Then, disaster strikes. A pie without sugar? How do you keep your face from reflecting that truth? Oh, to have heard the conversation that ensued that day! Be assured that <u>now</u>, Tess *always* asks Nana when being served a piece of any dessert if she remembered the sugar. Without that sticky, sweet ingredient, taste surely suffers! Pumpkin pie isn't even edible without sugar, just ask Tess.

Sugar sweetens, plain and simple. As with granulated sugar, it can fall like dry snow from the spoon into your coffee cup, your cereal bowl, or your half grapefruit to improve the final product and make the eating or drinking experience more palatable. But, brown sugar has something special about it, too. The "Baking Gods" have determined that this ingredient needs to be densely packed to be measured appropriately. It doesn't do a bit of good to pack granulated sugar tightly. Nothing makes it hold. However, brown sugar can be squeezed, molded, and formed. It can be pressed. It can be packed. It can be squished. Bakers push and press to get just as much as possible in the measuring cup, and recipes are made sweeter by the effort it takes.

I have one daughter who is a baker and really likes the kitchen and a second daughter who struggles to toast bread. I remember my younger daughter *attempting* a recipe once that called for brown sugar. I was loosely supervising from the other room, fully expecting a disaster in the kitchen, and hoping to steer clear from it all. I watched as she poured brown sugar from the Domino™ bag that she'd located in the pantry, measuring out one full measuring cup. She scraped the excess off onto the counter and poured the "precisely" measured sweetness into the mixing bowl.

"That's not how you do it," I yelled from the living room. I couldn't help myself. She couldn't understand. She was following the recipe, and nowhere did it read, "pack tightly." However, any experienced baker would know that brown sugar *always* has to be pressed down and packed tightly to be appropriately measured. Recipes are packed with a sweetness punch in this way.

Sweet friends are a blessing. They surely improve the recipe, don't they? Without them, we'd have to fake a smile at life because there would definitely be something missing from the recipe. And, if a woman thinks through her circle of influence, there are a few sweet friends that just carry a little extra of their goodness. They are densely packed with blessing, and it seems to be a joy for them to share it. They embody Luke 6:38, "If you give to others, you will be given a full amount in return. **It will be packed down,** shaken together, and spilling over into your lap. The way you treat others is the way you will be treated" (The Message). Brown sugar friends are packed densely. The blessings they give spill out. They are blessed because they bless. Their hugs are extra sweet. Their smile is extra warm. Their friendship is extra special. Paul had a brown sugar friend just like that, an encourager who added sweetness not only to Paul's life but to others as well. His name was Tychicus.

Tychicus is mentioned only five times in the New Testament. Two of those mentions describe him with the very same language: he is a "dear brother," a "faithful minister," and a "fellow servant" (Colossians 4:7 and Ephesians 6:21, New International Version). When Paul mentions Tychicus in his writings, he is preparing to send him to a church for the *express purpose* of encouraging the hearts of the believers. While we don't know much about Tychicus, he appears to have been a brown sugar friend of Paul's. Think on it. Paul speaks of him highly. He wants the churches he is writing to know how great his love is for this friend. He is "dear" and "faithful." He seems to be saying, "This friend of mine, Tychicus, is a gem. We've been through a lot together. He is true blue.

He's never left me but has faithfully ministered to me time and time again. I want to share him with you. I'm confident he'll comfort your hearts and encourage you just as he has encouraged me." Wouldn't it be amazing for a man like Paul to record something in history like that about us?

Whether mentioned 5 times or 25 times, I'm a Tychicus fan! Think about the awesome responsibility of being the mouthpiece for Paul, God's first true missionary to Asia. Think about the task of carrying out Paul's wishes. Think about the privilege of going to a people that needed some of your sweetness to encourage their hearts. Paul wanted Tychicus, specifically Tychicus, to carry the message. Why? Because Paul knew that Tychicus' personality and nature would spill out and variably run over into the lives of the new believers; they would be comforted. Life would be made sweeter.

Don't miss the nuance here that Tychicus was *sent*. His sweetness was needed somewhere foreign to him. He had the gift of encouragement, and Paul asked him to share it, but Tychicus himself didn't know the audience. Sometimes the brown sugars that sweeten our lives move in and then back out. They might not "stick closer than a brother," because, following Luke 6:38, their nature is to spill over and bless. That's why they are packed so tightly with gifts of the Holy Spirit. They are sent to bless. They do so, and then they may be called to move on and bless someone else somewhere else. Perhaps they are "short and sweet" in this way. Enjoy them for the time you have them. Think of them as your *extra* measure of sweetness.

Consider also that you may represent brown sugar in this life recipe of friends. If this season of your life has you rubbing elbows with someone who is here today but potentially gone tomorrow, maybe your job is to comfort her heart and encourage her now, for the time you spend together. Bring sweetness to her. Don't miss the opportunity. If your life is richly blessed, allow the Lord to use that blessing to spill out and touch the hearts of others—"pressed down, shaken together, and running over" (Luke 6:38, New International Version).

CHAPTER 5

Eggs

Eggs are binders. Just consider a meatloaf. Whether a fan of meatloaf or not, this culinary creation can't be a loaf at all without eggs. Eggs have the capacity to pull things together and hold them there. I'm not very good at making meatloaf myself. Perhaps that is why I choose not to make it for my family, but I do remember making meatloaf as a child in my mom's kitchen. The whole creation seemed to be pretty messy. Bread crumbs, onion, a pound of hamburger, an extensive amount of ketchup, and that runny, slimy ol' egg, all tossed in a bowl and mixed by hand, at least that is the way I remember it. The perfectly formed loaf was placed gently into the pan before it went into the oven, and by virtue of the binding action of the egg, it remained a perfectly formed loaf when you took it from the oven 45 minutes later.

Like that recipe, the cookie recipe for life described in these pages has the need for eggs, the ingredient that holds things together. Without eggs our cookies (and our healthy, put-together lives) would fall apart. The attribute is slightly different, though, than the binding action of salt, which we've talked about already. Think about the emotions that surface and the mind picture that is formed when we talk about something falling apart. Have you personally ever fallen apart? What did that feel like? I've been there. I remember a fight with my husband once that left me on the kitchen floor, sobbing. My daughter was very young at the time. She crawled to me on the floor and reached out to me with a confused look on her face. Even now, when I look back at that picture in my mind, the best description of the situation was that things had "fallen apart." The wheels had come off. Brokenness abounded. When you reach those pits, ladies, you don't need leader friends. Those salty, binding women are terrific at accomplishing at task and drawing people together to achieve a goal. But, in these broken moments, you need *emotionally connected* friends—eggs.

I remember some egg-like ladies in my past. When I was a young girl, I would occasionally accompany my family to my dad's family reunions. I say occasionally because it was pretty rare that his family would get together. Some large families have a planned summer rendezvous with a specific date, an agreed-upon place of meeting, etc. Everyone who comes knows what "Aunt Sally" will bring–her delicious potato salad. Everyone knows that "Uncle Fred" will tell the same old stories that you heard last summer. And, in my family, everyone knew that they would be greeted by Aunt Merle, the hugging aunt. Perhaps the same sort of aunt pinches cheeks or takes too many pictures at your family reunions. In our family, "that" aunt was the hugger. As soon as she saw you coming, she'd meet you at the door with a hug. Sometime during the conversations that day, she'd find a reason to hug you again, as she learned about some sort of good or exciting news that had befallen you since the last reunion. And, when you were set to leave, she wouldn't let you load the car without another hug. While I might not have been connected with Aunt Merle in any other way, I could pretty much be assured I had a friendly, emotionally-driven relative who wouldn't ever mind if I needed a hug. She'd definitely be there to give one.

I think of Aunt Merle when I read through the passage of scripture about Ruth and Naomi. Yes, they were family. Ruth had married into the family, and similarly, my Aunt Merle had married my Uncle Elvin and became a Lewis by name (although after as many years as they had been married, we thought of her as blood). Interestingly though, Naomi was Ruth's *mother-in-law.* Countless horror stories and jokes have been created about relationships with mothers-in-law. Perhaps that is why this relationship in the Old Testament as a model for eggs in our recipe is all the more interesting. Ruth and her sister-in-law Orpah had married the two sons of Naomi, who was a widow. Not only Naomi's husband, but also both of her sons died, leaving the three women in the opening chapter of the book of Ruth widows. Naomi is devastated. She is broken. She has "fallen apart." In her despair, she tells her daughters-in-law to leave her. She says, "Go back to your homelands. What do I have to give to you? I am simply bitter." Orpah, seemingly without hard feelings and perhaps even hesitantly, does just what Naomi has suggested. She leaves, peacefully, but she leaves. Who stays? Ruth.

The Message, a paraphrase of the Bible, tells the story best:

> "Orpah kissed her mother-in-law good-bye; but Ruth embraced her and held on. Naomi said, 'Look, your sister-in-law is going back home to live with her own people and gods; go with her.' But Ruth said, 'Don't force me to leave you; don't make me go home. Where you go, I go; and where you live, I'll live. Your people are my people, your God is my god; where you die, I'll die, and that's where I'll be buried, so help me God—not even death itself is going to come between us!'" (Ruth 1:14-17)

That is emotional connection: embracing, holding on, vowing to never leave. Ruth was better than "a good egg" here, she was the very binder that Naomi needed to keep from falling apart.

As women, many of us have had those "falling apart" moments. Maybe some are coming to mind; maybe some of your "egg" friends are starting to surface in your thoughts as well. I have a good friend, Jenny. We grew up together. I was rough and tumble as a girl, and that's exactly the type of friend I chose. On sunny, summer afternoons, Jenny would swing by on her three-wheeler (which was the pre-cursor in the 1980s to today's all-terrain vehicles, quads, or four-wheelers as we now know them), and we would race through the countryside together. We were 4-H girls, too. 4-H clubs may not be popular in some areas of the country, but in our neck of the woods, this youth organization that promoted farm-family living, conservation, and public service was well-supported and highly popular among young people. At some point, my family and Jenny's decided that hauling the two of us around to those monthly 4-H meetings was just too much, so they turned over the keys to the pick-up and told us to go on our own. Don't tell any authorities this, but I'm pretty sure Jenny and I were driving beat-up, farm pick-up trucks by age 12. As President and Vice President of the 4-H club, lofty titles for two country girls, we'd make it our pledge to move through formalities quickly. I remember plans we'd make in advance of those monthly meetings:

"Think we can conclude this meeting within 30 minutes tonight?"

"Sure."

"Let's get it over with so that we can do something a bit more fun."

Yep. We were rebels (smile).

We were bus buddies throughout grade school, too. I was a year older, so when I could legally drive, I'd drop by her house before school, saving her from the atrocities of bus riding: bumpy roads, foul language, and dust. When together, we would talk about boys. We would talk about our parents. We would talk about our dreams for the future. We would talk about everything. For many, many years, we were emotionally connected. And, that set the stage for adulthood.

Jenny has always picked up the phone to call me in a crisis—even now, 35 years later. A few years ago, she called, "Aim, I need to talk." And, we did, for hours. Jenny's life hasn't been an easy one. I haven't lived every step with her, but through her tragic car accident, her divorce, her mother's all-too-early death, and her dad's heart attack, I've been by her side because she needed me and because I know that I am her "egg." We're emotionally connected. When my caller ID shows Jenny's name, I am prepared to talk, for hours if necessary. And, I know that she would do the same for me.

Recently, my dad was diagnosed with cancer. I hadn't really thought to call Jenny. I suppose a part of me wanted to be independently strong, ready to face whatever battle was ahead. It didn't matter that I hadn't called Jenny. *She called me.* That's the essence of an emotionally connected friend. Their response isn't conditional upon your plea for help. Remember? Naomi was sending Ruth away! Emotionally connected friends say, "I am here. I'm not leaving." They physically or symbolically reach out to embrace you and hold on tight.

Ladies, don't be without an emotionally connected egg. At the point of falling apart, a woman needs a friend who can be there for her to embrace and hold on.

CHAPTER 6

Vanilla

Vanilla is, quite possibly, the most interesting ingredient in our recipes, both for our lives as women and for a remarkable chocolate chip cookie. Have you ever tasted vanilla? Try it once. If you are like me, you probably already have, perhaps in a moment of sheer curiosity. Vanilla ice cream is great. I love vanilla crème chocolates out of a Russell Stover box. Most of us have munched on a box of vanilla wafers at some point, whether as a child, or in a moment of weakness while staring into a nearly empty pantry for a one-bite midnight snack. So, who could resist just a taste, a mere drip on your index finger, placed gingerly on the tip of your tongue? Ack! How could this seemingly wonderful flavoring be so misleading? Rarely does *anything* bearing the name vanilla disappoint me (cupcakes, milkshakes, pudding, fudge), but with plain, old vanilla, straight from the bottle, I'm very disappointed. It is bitter, very bitter, and not at all appetizing when tasted alone.

Another thing that has always intrigued me about vanilla: vanilla cake mixes, vanilla wafers, vanilla crème...what color are they? White, of course. So, why is the bottle of vanilla flavoring in the pantry always dark, almost black? This necessary ingredient in our recipe is not only bitter to taste, but it is dark, and that doesn't at all sound like a good combination. In fact, those qualities sound scary and distasteful all together. When likening our life recipe to the ingredients in our cookie, we have to ask ourselves, "Why would I want to welcome someone into this personal space of mine that is scary, dark, bitter, and potentially distasteful?" Let's explore an excellent reason; we'll start with a scripture.

Proverbs 27:17 says, "As iron sharpens iron, so one person sharpens another" (New International Version). The black-to-white quality of vanilla is rather interesting in light of this scripture. If no one were around to keep us sharp, we'd believe our own way of looking at the world was spot-on. This is black, and that is white. It is when we are rubbed just a little, thrown off by a comment or an alternate way of thinking, that we begin to recognize maybe life isn't as neat and predictable as we believe. Maybe some of our rough edges need adjustment. And, what is the best sharpening stone? Something just as hard, feisty, and tough as we are as women—another woman!

Take a moment to consider who might be your feisty friend in your circle of acquaintances and comrades, and as you do, I'll share a story about mine. Often, when I talk with others about this ingredient in life's recipe, I refer to my daughter, Belle. She is my vanilla. She gives my life flavor and enhances who I am, but sometimes I lose focus on how flavorful I am becoming because of her, and I want to change the nature of who she is instead. At times, what I see in her (not to my credit) is her "dark side" and her "bitterness." They distract me from the flavorful end product, which is her gift to me, as she makes me a better mom and a better Christian.

A few years ago, Belle and I were driving home from a basketball game. She had just participated in an after-season game on a Sunday night. We'd driven quite a distance together to get to the gymnasium where she'd played. After talking through the game on our way back, the atmosphere in the car was pretty quiet. I thought all had been said. Then, Ms. Vanilla spoke up. She said to me, "Mom, will you evaluate me?" Somewhat confused because we'd already commented for miles about the game, I asked, "You mean about how you played tonight?" She was quick to respond, "No. I mean about life. How am I doing?" **She was 12 at the time.** 12! What 12-year-old asks a question of her mother like that? I believe I was a bit dumbfounded. I don't know that I remember a single word I said to her that night. I'll bet she remembers, though. Why do I think so? I believe that because in the follow-up conversation, I asked her to evaluate me. And her response to me that night I remember well. We both needed to *hear* the other person. The verse in Proverbs about iron sharpening iron is a mental image for what happened that night in the car. In those moments, her words to me were like the needed force of a grinding stone. As I listened, I could feel the abrasiveness of her sentiments, they were sharpening me. As she spoke, I could recognize the truth in what she was saying and knew this was a conversation that would be for my own good.

She said, "Well, I wish that you would use scripture to teach me more often." Ugh. "You mean the way I am parenting you isn't good or not good enough?" I remember thinking. Give me a break, child. You aren't the easiest child to parent! Wait until you walk a day in the shoes of a worn-out, working mom, then you'll see that there just isn't enough energy left to be the mom you think I need to be. The thoughts continued down this path for a while, but I didn't let them roll off my lips. Soon, The Lord opened my eyes and my heart to my vanilla, sitting right there beside me in the car that night. There she sat, not combative, not placing blame, not really even criticizing, just telling me what she needed from me as her mama. Suffice it to say that nowadays I try to leave a few notes on her bed here and there with a scripture for her to read and consider. She responds to those well, I've learned. When I hear a poignant sermon and she is sitting by my side, I'll take the time to discuss it with her later, sharing my take-aways and asking what hers were. I'm sharper now, and she made me that way.

Fast-forward a few years. I was traveling with my own mom to a ladies tea where I had been asked to share a message about our lives as women and our friendship needs. I'd been traveling and speaking for various groups for a while, but my mom had never listened to me speak about the chocolate chip cookie model. She was happy to be there and participated that afternoon with all of the ladies assembled.

I asked the ladies to document *exactly who* in their lives represented these various ingredients. Who is your brown sugar? Who is your salt? And so on. From my vantage point in the front of the room, I recognized that my mom was writing down names as I moved through the recipe, as were the other listeners. My mom and I talked about the event a bit on our way home that afternoon. She said to me, "You made my list." I said, "I did, huh?" She responded, "Yep. Would you like to know what ingredient you are?" I was pretty sure I had this one nailed because not only do my daughter Belle and I physically look much alike, we are kindred spirits. I said, "I know which one I am. I'm your vanilla." I was. I am. I probably always will be to her.

Don't push away those who make you sharper. Don't see her as an unnecessary friend who only introduces challenges or seems less than tasty at times. She is there for a purpose, and as women, we need her. She's vanilla; life will have greater flavor with her than without.

CHAPTER 7

Butter

I imagine I was nine or ten years old when the first microwave oven was introduced to our home. My dad purchased it as a Christmas gift for my mom. In later years, I would learn that the purchase of any gift that plugs into a wall socket is likely not the right purchase for a husband to his wife, but this was different. This was cutting edge! At that time, who knows just how much it cost, but I remember it being an elaborate gift that year. It was far too big to go under the tree. It had to be "hidden" on the porch, the front entrance to our home that no one ever used. The box alone was big enough to create a cardboard fort for my brother and me to play in, which was likely our greater joy that day than any convenience this new appliance would bring, like thawing meat quickly, reheating leftovers, or popping microwave popcorn. What third grader could appreciate a microwave oven? What fun could that be? I'm glad my name wasn't on that gift tag, regardless of the size of the box.

However, there was one convenience of the microwave that I marveled at: melting butter. As I had watched my mom bake in the kitchen all the years prior, I knew only one method for melting butter. One had to unwrap the stick, place it in a saucepan, and watch it melt slowly, from the bottom up, on the electric range. But, melting butter in the microwave, oh, this was surely different, and fun to watch. I *wanted* to help with this task. I would remove the paper from the stick of buttery goodness, place it in a "microwave-safe" bowl (a phrase that took some time and trial to effectively understand), cover it with waxed paper to prevent a messy clean-up later, and stand back in awe. The melting of that stick was unpredictable. As the turntable rotated, it was as if lasers were shooting radioactive beams into the yellow-tinted ingredient. You might see the middle of the stick begin to cave. And, then, toward the end of one side, you'd see the corner start to lose its shape, collapsing under the laser's power. A puddle formed at the bottom of the bowl, but not across the entire surface area, only where special forces had been at work. Finally, leave the stick in long enough, and the end result was exactly what happened on the stove, except that it wouldn't have been nearly as fun to watch. Watching butter melt in the microwave: in the early 80s, that was exciting and a marvel of the kitchen! It was new, uncharted territory in the cooking experiences of my home.

This new-fangled laser box would be instrumental in chocolate chip cookie recipes, too. Commonly, the directions to such simple dessert treats read, "soften butter." Whether we choose to use a microwave or a simple saucepan and range top, butter must be transformed just a little before it is ready to use in our cookie creation. This is significant. When a substance is melted, it more easily covers. Straight from the refrigerator, you can unwrap a half cup of butter and drop the stick into your mixing bowl, but its effect on the other ingredients is changed when it can be <u>poured</u> over the entire concoction. The way it *covers* everything is much like prayer.

Many of us have used the phrase or have found comfort in knowing that we are "covered in prayer." Peacefulness comes in imagining the prayers of friends and family. Personal prayers form a blanket of protection, gently covering us, protecting us from harm, giving us comfort and warmth, and establishing a barrier between us and all of the evils that surround us. Not long ago, while reading a devotion I came across this question, "Who is praying for you?" I had to pause. It was much easier for me to answer the question, "Who are you praying for?" I could rattle off names, circumstances, and situations that had filled my prayer time. I could go to my prayer journal where I documented petitions raised for healing, safety, guidance, direction, and peace for many, *and by name. That* task was so much easier for me. That question I could answer with ease. But to know that someone is praying for me? That was a trickier subject.

When ladies are able to list their prayer requests, document their prayer times, schedule devotions, and synchronize their calendars to accommodate small group meetings among their other responsibilities, they show Type-A personality traits. Type-A folks take charge and are generally meticulously organized. These ladies establish a plan and see it through. If you are raising your hand as if to say, "that's me," I'm with you. It is so much easier for us to be doers. We stay on task, make lists, and check off our completions. "Sure, I'll pray for you. I'd be honored." Type-A folks can speak these words with confidence and promise. But, to open our lives to the degree that we expose needs and place heartfelt requests into the hands of another who would lift those issues up on our behalf...that is a pretty scary thought to an independent "doer."

Those of us who are self sufficient know we need someone's words to touch the throne of heaven so that a blanket of peace and *melted* tranquility falls on us. (Remember that stick of butter?) But, as strong, independent souls, we find it easier to be a part of the prayer-covering process in the lives of others. We might crave stillness and peace in the presence of The Lord, but we hesitate to draw close enough to another to feel the kind of spiritual coverage this type of fellowship can give. To some degree, we all resist such intimacy with another woman whom we can trust our secrets and expose our needs. Is her prayer on our behalf worth the risk? We question. Acknowledging this necessity, though, is critical. Identify the butter in your life. She's the one waiting to approach the throne with our secret concerns. She's the one who is on her knees in her prayer closet for you and for me. She will cover us with prayer, if we will let her.

Sometimes when we draw close enough to a buttery friend, mutual intercession just comes naturally. I've been able to find this with my friend, Lori. Lori is a hard-working, sacrificial, single mom. When I met her in 2011, her one and only son, the love of her life, was a high school junior and highly capable in his sport of choice: wrestling. Lori's whole life revolved around her son. She dreamed with him of turning his passion for wrestling into a full-time job—whether professional or coaching. Together, they had overcome all odds, never relying upon food stamps or government subsidies, even though she qualified. Now, he was two years from leaving the nest, using his strengths to fly forward, and exiting this boyhood portion of his life. When I met Lori, acknowledging this fact was like a dagger to her heart. So much pain fills this stage of life for both mother and son. Who was she without him? How could she ever, as a single mom, support him financially through college? What would these next few years look like?

Lori shared these fears with me in the Bible study times we had together. She often shed a few tears as she spoke about financial struggles, emotional struggles, and identity struggles. But, this was always in privacy. To everyone else, Lori was a bubbly personality type. Her laughter rang through the office building, and her smile lit the room, but I knew I had a special place in Lori's life because she allowed me to see her pain. She shared with me her needs. She trusted me to pray on her behalf. I was her butter. My job was to cover her in prayer as I approached the throne of the peace-giver.

One day in particular she came bouncing into my office. A college her son had considered attending had contacted her to offer him a sizable wrestling scholarship! Her eyes were welling with tears as she shared her joy with me. She said, "I can't imagine why they would call and offer something like this now." I smiled and reached for the spiral-bound prayer journal that sat on the edge of my desk. Completely overwhelmed with what I knew was happening, I trembled as I thumbed through the pages. I proceeded to flip to the entry that I had penned *that very morning*. It read, "Lord, please bless Lori with an unexpected financial blessing." As I read those words, she rounded my desk to give me a hug. Both of us stood sobbing in that moment, knowing that God had moved in a powerful and mighty way for us to feel, to see, to appreciate, and to benefit. I had the privilege of covering my friend in prayer. She was blessed. I think I was blessed just as much, if not more.

Butter is vital in your recipe. It represents exposure. It represents trust. It represents a peace that cannot be known unless you can answer affirmatively, "Yes, I know my friend, _____, is praying for me. And, I couldn't do without her." Find that prayer warrior and trust her to cover you.

CHAPTER 8
Chocolate Chips

I have a recipe in my card arsenal that is simply labeled, "Cookies." It is a beat-up, old index card, and the juvenile hand-writing would suggest that I penned the recipe when I was about 10 years old. Perhaps this was when I had just started adding cards to the file that I'll now hand down to my own children. I likely copied it verbatim from my mom's recipe, housed alphabetically in her dingy, forest green recipe card file. Literally, the recipe is all about the dough. At the bottom of the card, the instructions say to add any of the following: 1 cup of chocolate chips, 1 cup of coconut, 1 cup of raisins, 1 cup of dates, or 1 cup of oatmeal. The choice is yours as the master baker in your kitchen. In all of the years that I have pulled this card from the file and assembled the ingredients, I don't remember a time when my choice for completing the recipe **wasn't** with chocolate chips.

Don't let the existence of a recipe box or an "arsenal of recipes" fool you. I am not a master chef or a master baker. When I ask my family what I can fix for them on a special occasion (birthday, last day of school, all A's on a report card), I generally get a strange look and a request for some restaurant in town. Despite the fact that I love to be in the kitchen, maybe it's not the place where my family loves to see me.

To solidify this argument, I submit my experiences with a phenomenon in the Midwest known as the "pot luck" or the infamous "pitch in." In South Central Illinois, church members, office mates, and other assemblies of people often collaborate to host a shared feeding at an overloaded feeding trough. Filling the galley of tables (generally the white, plastic variety) strewn end to end are dishes of all types and categories. Meats, casseroles, side dishes, salads, desserts, appetizers, and more are jammed as tightly as one can squeeze them. Organizers will attempt to put the meatier portions of the meal toward the front end of the table where Hefty® paper plates are stacked several inches tall. (They must be Hefty® because generic paper plates will never be able to withstand the weight of the food that will soon be piled in much-too-large portions on top of them.) Gradually, as one moves to the end of the table, offerings include side dishes, then salads, then desserts. After the meal has been served and the clean-up has begun, the task no cook EVER wants is to retrieve a dish that is still untouched. Either by sheer appearance or smell alone, this is the dish that has been deemed inedible by all of the passers-by as they pick and choose their portions for the event. The "untouchable" dish will now need to be taken home by some woman in shame. She'd literally rather leave it there unclaimed than apologetically admit to God and all assembled that, "Yes, this was my dish. I'm sorry." Guess who has been *that* woman on more than one occasion? Sadly, me.

Perhaps it is because I have taken my lumps and learned the hard way, but I would *never* try to sneak one cup of raisins in my generic "cookie" recipe in exchange for one cup of chocolate chips. In my household, that would be un-American and also uneaten. I've also learned that I cannot just include one cup of *any old* chocolate chips. Brand name is of no importance to my sweets-loving family, but if I don't pick up a bag of **semi-sweet** chips at the store, then I can promise there'll be a bit of a ruckus and maybe even some "inedibles" left on the plate. In our household, milk chocolate chips just will not do. "They are too sweet," my husband will say. Semi-sweet chips just make for better cookies. Too much sweetness ruins the recipe for us.

This gives me pause as I consider the chocolate chip cookie analogy. Previous chapters have pointed to just the right persons offering just the right mix for just the right combination—your dough. You need women of salt. You need the bitter taste of vanilla. You need the binding power of eggs. You need the fullness of soda. But the recipe concludes with chocolate chips, an ingredient that life will supply without asking and without permission. Plenty of chips will fall into the batter, awaiting the mixing of a wooden spoon. Some of them are, at best, only *semi*-sweet. Let me offer a few: a wedding, the birth of a child, a promotion, a new home, a dream vacation, the death of a parent, a car accident, the loss of a job, the disintegration of a marriage, bankruptcy, cancer. How do we become women who, by the grace of God, can say, "Let the chips fall where they may?"

Examine what happens when chocolate chips fall from the bag of experience into life's bowl. Isn't their landing softened just a bit by the ingredients that have been made ready to receive them? Whether sprinkled gingerly or dumped without hesitation into the batter, the dough is prepared, ready to absorb the avalanche of the chocolate. Grab any chocolate chip recipe. What ingredient is the last to be added? The chips. All of the ingredients have been assembled with care, and together they form a pillow of batter upon which the chips may drop— whether violently or delicately.

Dough is prepared first for a reason. Chips poured upon hot, melted butter alone would likely cause the chips to melt. What kind of cookie would result from melted chips? Chips poured on flour alone could be stirred endlessly, but, by themselves, flour and chips will never be cohesive. This is all elementary, but you get the point. Life's chips will fall. Concentrate not upon them, milky or semi-sweet; concentrate upon the platform where they will be received—the place where you have prepared a doughy mix of friends to help absorb the experience.

As women, it is easy to set our focus upon the one ingredient in this life that is certain: uncertainty. Life <u>is</u> unpredictable. Why not just embrace that? I can no more tell you what will happen tomorrow than can a seer like Nostradamus. James was clear about what we can and cannot know when he wrote the following: "Now listen, you who say, 'Today or tomorrow we will go to this or that city, spend a year there, carry on business and make money.' Why, you do not even know what will happen tomorrow. What is your life? You are a mist that appears for a little while and then vanishes." (James 4:13-14, New International Version). How do we learn from that? How do we keep ourselves from fearing the future?

I've admired women who take life's lumps in stride, letting the chips fall where they may. I give a measure of esteem to ladies who have pushed through the glass ceiling at their workplace, suffered through breast cancer and won, struggled to raise an autistic child with honor and grace, survived the sting of an unfaithful husband, or have overcome the hurt of miscarriage and infertility. We all know women just like this and marvel at their strength. Where do they get that kind of toughness and grit? Undeniably it is from The Lord, but each of those same women likely surrounded herself with Godly people who helped her absorb it all. Let's not set our minds on the chips. Let them fall because, whether we like it or not, they will. Instead, prepare the dough. We need to prepare our networks of friends and family. When we gather women around us in just the right measure, we are ready to withstand. The batter, that pillow of softness combined from common ingredients in just the right amounts, is the stuff of sweetness **and** strength.

CHAPTER 9

Apply Heat and Pressure

If it is truly all about the dough, then what more is there to this model for the fellowship among women? Who hasn't craved a spoonful of dough (ok, maybe a whole bowlful) short of it actually reaching the oven? Is there necessity to heat and pressure? Let me offer a story that distinctly answers, "yes."

In the late 1990s, my view of my own life was bliss. I had grown up in a very Godly home with Christian parents who modeled righteousness. I had married my high school sweetheart, who accepted The Lord soon after we started dating. What middle-aged woman can talk about the devotions she studied with the love-of-her-life at 17 years of age or the memories of going on church choir tour together? When we finished college, we both secured good jobs, and after spending a few years renting, we built our own place in a neighborhood where I could see us raising a small family and settling down for a lifetime of blessing and joy. We were healthy. We were educated. We had a wonderful church family and friends that enhanced our lives both as a couple and individually. Truly, life was bliss. Had I taken inventory at that time of those women with whom I surrounded myself, I feel certain that I could have identified eggs, flour, sugar, vanilla, soda, and everything else that would make the recipe complete; it was certainly a tasty life. However, in a moment of weakness or genius (to this day I'm not sure which, although I know it was ordained thought), I prayed a prayer that would change life forever.

With a 40-minute commute to and from my home to my office, Christian radio was a perfect means to relax and unwind. I could not tell you who spoke the words that day in the car, but I can still hear the question repeated over and over and over: *"Are you broken?"* It wasn't a question that was meant to address those who *knew* they were broken. The forcefulness of the phrase, the repetition, the context of the question all seemed much more suited to ears like mine. I was the one enjoying bliss. I was the one awaiting more prosperity and richness in life. I was the one excited to go home to my husband and continue in my happy world. I was, perhaps, a bit perplexed by the question and somewhat agitated. Was I broken? No! But the point this poignant and forever-remembered speaker was making to me was that I SHOULD BE BROKEN. In that moment, I realized that my life of bliss represented the <u>absence</u> of heat and pressure. My happy-go-lucky world might not be allowing me to realize God's fullness and His promise to be "more than enough." The speaker that day went on to say, "I couldn't trust a man who has not been broken."

Untrustworthy? That statement crossed a line with me. Surely I was trustworthy. After all, take a look at my history. I was raised a Christian. I had led others to Christ. I had followed the upright path. I was a virgin when married to my high school sweetheart. I attended church all of my life...even through those college years when it seems *everyone* turns away and reassesses their need for God. At 20-something years of age, I was proud of my <u>whole</u>someness. No, I was not broken. I never had been. Yet, in the space of one radio broadcast, I started to question all of that. Should I be broken? *Shouldn't* I be broken?

What was there to do in that moment but pray? With my eyes fully opened, as I drove that used, high-mileage commuter car down Highway 10 in Central Illinois, I prayed, "Lord, break me." Within a short 40-minute commute, this one speaker, God love him, had convinced me that I was missing so much in my life because God wanted to become more to me. I **needed** brokenness. I **needed** a story. I **needed** to be laid low to take hold of the truth that He was my everything. I **needed** some heat and pressure because my life in the mixing bowl, all put together with the right ingredients, wasn't enough. In fact, it was not even close.

In the years that followed, I would find out just how much God could be in the midst of brokenness. I suffered a miscarriage (in fact, this was within only days of the car ride) I then went through a period of infertility. My husband turned away from God in those days because he, too, had this dream of a beautiful young family in a brand new home stretched over an acre of land in a special little spot in DeWitt County, Illinois. When that dream seemed fractured, he blamed God. Of course, I suppose he could have blamed me. After all, I had prayed the prayer. In my heart, I knew exactly what had started this avalanche.

As a young husband and wife, we then fell into debt, extreme debt. We struggled mightily in our marriage, to the degree that holding it together was about all that we could do at one point. We suffered through job loss and relocation. We questioned our faith. We gained and lost friends. To package it all simply: we experienced a brokenness that neither of us had ever known before in 20 years of living.

Think about the recipe again. Specifically, see yourself standing over the mixer, ensuring that the dry ingredients in your perfect cookie concoction effectively compliment the wet ingredients. You scrape the sides of the bowl as the beaters whip around and around. In a split second, perhaps you lose control of the spatula, and it becomes entangled in those beaters. You have to immediately reach for the stop button to make sure you don't cause damage. In that instant, you are scared about how powerful this machine is in your hands. What if that mixer had pulled in not only your spatula, but a finger? I remember fearing this as a mom when I taught my eldest daughter to bake. All of that pressure is a bit scary, but it is also effective. The nine ingredients in your recipe sitting side by side in the stainless steel mixing bowl were the perfect measurements, readied for the most perfect, simplistic dessert, but without a real beating, they're not ready. They need pressure. They need whipped, knocked around, and broken apart so that their effectiveness and their unique properties can be made to work collectively. They are being united for submission to the *Refiner's* fire (Malachi 3), where what will emerge is purified. Where does that happen? In a heated oven.

Preheat oven to 350ºF. Those words precede recipe upon recipe, cookies or otherwise. We know it is coming. No cookie-baker expects to leave the kitchen with prize-winning cookies if the oven stays cold. That's why this direction—preheat oven—is quite generally the first instruction given. I've occasionally been under a time-crunch to get a dessert baked before I rush off to a ball game, a dinner with friends, or a church potluck and in my hurry, I have failed to follow the very first, important instruction: PREHEAT. Ugh! I know it needs to bake; of course it needs to bake. In our lives as women, we would be better served if we remembered that this instruction is often the first one, so be prepared.

Things are going to have to get hot for ingredients to work effectively together. As a young girl, I often observed the crafts and handiwork of my grandparents. A common card table covered with ceramics and a rainbow of colorful paints from which to choose sat in their darkened and damp basement. It was a magical place to me. My grandma had a cousin who was an expert craftsman, and together this family of handymen and women would produce some of the most beautiful works of art. My mom still displays a gorgeous nativity set at Christmas completed by their very talented hands. The vibrant blankets draped over the camels intricately match the wardrobes of the three wise men. The angel's wings glisten. The expression on Mary's face is priceless, and the cattle and sheep are lifelike with their perfected shadows and colorings.

I know little of the process for creating these ceramic masterpieces. I'm sure at the time I was too rambunctious and uncaring to understand or appreciate the process. I can only remember that the white and chalky figurines to be painted were fragile and that I could not play with them. And, although layers of perfectly matched paints beautified these collectibles, nothing made them more impressive than the kiln at my cousin Agnes' house, where Mimmie and Pappy would take the painted works to have them "fired." This process, this atmosphere, this extreme heat changed everything about Mary Poppins' wall hangings, Donald Duck banks, nativity sets, salt and pepper shakers, and any other ceramic ware that had come from my grandparent's tiny basement. The kiln made those works awesome...vibrant, bright, shiny, strong, and presentable as gifts or goods for sale. As much as I liked how a collectible jewelry box with an image of Cinderella looked when it sat in that basement, the final product was MUCH more beautiful. Even I could learn to wait on the end product when I knew that the firing process would showcase amplified beauty of the piece. And, I wouldn't need to worry as much about the weakness of the material after it was fired either. That kiln changed everything.

What did I learn from those ceramics? It was OK to apply heat. It was *good* to apply heat. Too often, even though we have prepared for the process by preheating, we are scared by that same extreme temperature. It burns. It is dangerous. Its power frightens us. May I just suggest that its power to beautify and strengthen is far more worthy and significant? It is simply <u>worth it</u> to see the final product. That dough that you have meticulously assembled needs a beautification system. It needs a process to burn away the imperfections and solidify the remains. Your dough needs an oven. It needs the Refiner's fire. Enter the flames boldly because what emerges in the end is gorgeous, strong, and worthwhile.

CHAPTER 10

Your Life. Your Dough.

If only life proceeded so simply. I'd love to be assured that the instructions for what to assemble, hand-written on a flimsy, dog-eared index card would produce a perfect dessert. But, too often I've followed recipes to the letter and yet ended up with nothing more than a flop to serve to my family...just ask them. It really isn't that easy. It really isn't that simple.

Christ said, "I have come so that everyone would have life, and have it in its fullest" (John 10:10, Contemporary English Version). His desire is to see us enjoying this world that He has created. Our lives are gifts, and it is our privilege to enjoy them to the fullest. Surround yourself, ladies of God, with ingredients to perfect the dough...the stuff of life. Work at it. And, recognize not all of it will be pleasant. Occasionally, a bad egg is in the dozen. Sometimes the baking soda sat in the pantry too long, and the date stamped on the bottom of the box shows it is expired. Once in a while, you simply measure wrong. But, practice makes perfect. Life is to be lived to the fullest. Once you know the recipe, continue to follow, follow, follow until you're full, full, full. God bless.

Printed in the United States
By Bookmasters